Date Due

THE GRACE OF PRIVATE PASSAGE

The Grace of Private Passage

Karen Mulhallen

Black Moss Press
2000

Published by Black Moss Press, 2450 Byng Road, Windsor, Ontario N8W 3E8, Canada. Black Moss books are distributed in Canada and the U.S. by Firefly Books.

Black Moss Press would like to acknowledge the support of the Canada Council for the Arts for its publishing program, along with the help given by the Ontario Arts Council this year.

Canadian Cataloguing In Publication Data

Mulhallen, Karen
   The grace of private passage

Poems.
ISBN 0-88753-340-X

I. Title

PS8756.U4147G736.2000   C811'.54   C00-900315-0
PR9199.3.M76G73 2000

Acknowledgements:
Versions of some of these poems have appeared in The Malahat Review, The Antigonish Review and Salmagundi.
Both "The Caverns of Ely" and "Herm on Tour" were published as chapbooks by Pasdeloup Press (1997 and 1998)
"The Mouse in the Cinderella Pageant" appeared in *That Sign of Perfection, Poems and Stories on the Game of Hockey*, and "Your Big Nose Etcetera" was published in *I Want to be the Poet of Your Kneecaps, Poems of Quirky Romance*, each edited by John B. Lee (Black Moss Press, 1995 and 1999)
Grateful acknowledgement is made to the Hawthornden Castle International Writers' Retreat, Hawthornden Castle, Lasswade, Scotland, where the Australian and Scottish poems in this collection were conceived.
The cover image is after a tempera painting by John Duncan, *St Bride*, (1913), and is reproduced here with the permission of the National Gallery of Scotland, Edinburgh.

For Beth Bentley
and
For Nancy Huston

Contents

I

Antipodean Suite

Antipodes: *Those having the feet opposite. Those who dwelt directly opposite to each other on the globe, as it were feet against feet. Those who in any way resemble the dwellers on the opposite side of the globe. Places on the surface of the earth directly opposite to each other, or the place which is directly opposite to another. The exact opposite of a person or thing.*

Suite: *A train of followers, attendants, or servants. A number of rooms forming a set used by a person, a family or a company of persons. A set of furniture of uniform pattern. A series of dance tunes arranged for one or more instruments and composed in the same key or related keys. A sequel, result, in agreement of harmony. Of rooms: in a series leading from one to the other.*

I. Woolpack Farm. Boorowa

After we hoisted you up on the horse,
myself on the Welsh pony, Short Black,

Ross high in the saddle of his crazy beauty,
Karla the roan,

Jerry on the great chestnut stallion,
you on Molly, the sweet sorrel bay

when you bolted away up the hill
leaving behind only a trail

of girlish laughter, I tried
to gather your pearly giggles

as they flew, restring
the necklace of delight

marvelled at your gallop:
Hold tight now. Go on, Go on.

II. Canberra

I have to tell you how it touched me
to fasten up your thick long hair.
And your shoes. My hand on the shoehorn.
Tying the laces. And the lifting up of clothes to the line,

Pegging them against the wind, which
in Canberra blows always, and
especially in autumn, which
is our spring. A thousand small things,

little domestic moments, a counter
wiped, a bathtub rinsed, stove
scoured, and the clothes folded
from the line. For me, it was nothing to bend

to pick up coins from the floor,
to carry trash to the bins,
hoist a bag, reach a box,
button a blouse, adjust the back

on an earring. Small, but not so small
the privilege of intimacy has its own
huge scale. And we are graced
without contrivance when it falls.

III.Boorowa

In the photographs on the station at Boorowa
you have a bottle raised to your lips.
You are wearing a hat, a silly hat,

I bought in Cairns, and the horses
are at the ready by the shed.
You are small in the photographs,

smaller than in life
brown tail down your back, head up,
chin to the clouds, bottle held aslant.

What did I want to say
about that moment catching you?
Did I wonder if it was water or wine?

Did I look about for the remnants
of the feast? Had we broken
bread together?

IV. On Board The Beagle

That first weekend we travelled
like a congerie of bees
Braidwood, Bateman's Bay, Beagle Bay.
We caught the sun falling on the Tasman Sea
     rapturous as the gulf islands
sailed in to view
          ate fish and chips from paper packets
          slept braced by sea air
while our neighbours performed a ritual barbecue.

In the brief compass of a single day
   we swam against the currents
   explored tidal pools, and watched
   roos romping in a forest glade.

You, our muse, eager on the beach,
     you joined the fray
urged us on to more, and more
   the first to plunge into the waves,
   to climb the dunes, to free the molluscs
     to greet the tides.

Bent, you were still the girl in bud, Beth
still in bathing suit, high heels and baton
emerging from the west
a whole new world before you
that whole new world you gave to us.

V. The Great Barrier Reef

Afloat on the Coral Sea, I left behind
my rage at your illness, its unjust ways.
Immersed in slender schools translucent
grey and yellow jack fish, I rode

the backs of graceful sea turtles,
astride currents of cold and of warmth
like Gulliver tiny cowering beneath
a six hundred pound Maori wrasse

giant brown and green flourescent
lips opening at my face,
towered over delicate Halloween
orange and black clown fish dancing

in the fingers of silky coral anemones.
The sea was alive with fluttering green fans
red gorgonian tree corals, shocking blue
brain corals, orange tube corals, purple

leaf corals, giant sheets, plates and
delicate ivory trees. I floated
head down, sideways, flipping
over and over, cut free of time

and space, hanging on angles,
in a watery Manhattan.
Heaven, said the divemaster,
you looked like you were in heaven.

La Sirena. Serena. And I was.

VI. Morning Beyond Baron Gorge

One day I left my submarine Paradise
      for the old mining town of Kuranda

through open eucalyptus woods
      to wet green screens and massive

fig trees aching with the chatter of birds
reaching up to towering Kauri pines.

High above the rainforest canopy
stretched the green and yellow fronds

delicate pink tube flowers creamy mouthed
Lawyer canes. Orchids and ferns clung

to the trees. Through the carpet a glint of river, gorge
falls and the shy white flightless Cassoway bird.

Down Coondoo street a parliament of creatures
unfolds toward Saint Saviour's Bush Pole Bell Tower.

A charming spiny-quilled echidna escaped
from its hamburger-honeyed feeding tube

extends its body-long tongue, out of its beak
searching for juicy ants.

Fruit bats and sugar gliders perch on each
of my shoulders, display their furry capes

parachuting from tree to tree.
Fat bush- and ring-tailed oppossums

blink at the bright sunshine
humming, chattering, banging on sticks

14

as they hang from my outstretched arms.
A tiny shy grey wallaby, miniature roo,

hopped in the lead by the side of a lumbering
cuddly dirty-bummed blunt-headed wombat.

The caged walls of the noctarium crumbled
the aluminium girdered butterfly sanctuary

turned to dust as thousands of butterflies
fluttered out in the fresh bright damp

morning air. There were
flowers everywhere:

lace, tube, bottle-brush, cylinder, bugle-shaped
pinks, roses, whites, golds, and mauves

and my Arcadian friends sipping
on nectar, festooned with garlands,

stumbled, waddled, glided, fluttered
down Main Street toward the old

wooden church, its louvred walls open
to greet us. The wooden lectern

shaped like a butterfly moved
in a cloud of soft colour, as one

then another, then another
butterfly alighted there.

The altar worked like walnut, mahoganny-figured,
rough grained local wood, was alive

with caterpillars beginning to pupate.
On the seats of pews soft with golden fluffy flower balls,

eucalyptus leaves, fuzzy grey koalas
irritably shoved, and pushed, and lolled

as up from the crypt to the croak
of cicadas, and the squawking sulphur-crested cockatoos,

flew a crowd of green budgerigars, soft grey rose-breasted
galahs, and the bright red flash of rosellas.

A cheer went up above the laughter of kookaburras
as the creatures all raised their voices

a commotion of flashy green warblers
the insistent tenor of black and white magpies

as the caterpillars dropped their mouths
grew antennae, divided their legs

pads became wings, eyes
arranged for technicolour

and the beating of brilliant blue
air pulsating, a million velvet petals

amid soft lemon flowers, calling
the living, and summoning all to the grave.

VII. Captain Cook's Crescent

If I were to try to tell anyone
  of what it was in particular
about that journey to see you
  so far away

If I could find the words
that held the pain and closeness
of discovering
you laughing like a schoolgirl

at dawn beside piles of receipts for your taxes
while Jerry and I slept through the night
of the bounty of braiding up your golden tresses
of the sorrow of soil in the small washbasin

of the tender shoehorning over tight joints and bunions
of the seat belt's buckle
of the jade studs in your ears
of tucking in to the back of your tunic

the escaped label, its washing instructions
hanging upside down
between the clear curves of your shoulder blades.

VIII. Canberra Airport

It's hard to explain the feeling
of seeing you standing there
by your motorized chair
in the Botannic Gardens

on the sun and shadowed lawn
surrounded by eucalyptus
squinting up to the sun
in the bright morning light

waving at my camera eye.
And it's impossible to tell how
it moved me, that last day together,
when you rose or fumbled or stumbled

out of your bed, in the grey of the pre-dawn light
and put on your flowered blouse
and your earrings of stiff gold-veined flowers
dipped in molten glass

and your Queensland raffia hat
to come to the little airport
to watch me pass the security gates
as the sun rose and spread

across the wet tarmac.

IX. Tidbinbilla

At Tidbinbilla we watched the vibrant bower birds
brilliant red rosellas and white sulphur-crested cockatoos mass at feed-
ing
swoop down at the gamekeeper

squabble squawk flee
a lone duck dove and dove and dove
a perfect pike, splash, slide, slither and up.

Jerry and I took to the Hills, the yellow and red Trails,
searching for koalas on the topmost boughs
you and your stick left behind.

Deep in the forest we went awkward
down banks for duck-billed platypus and wobbly ant-eaters
up gorges to the clatter of birds, prodding for soft

little long-snouted bilbies
until suddenly in a fork in a glade
you were there.

Through grasslands and banksia
long cylinders of golden flower spikes ribbed with red styles
300 year old grass trees, moist gullies

open forest, we strolled for the lyre bird
lept large granite boulders,
forest of ribbon and mountain gums

following the winding wet walk
to cascading mountain streams
echidnae and platypus all our care

yet not forgotten the reason we were there.

X. The National Gallery

By the shores of Lake Burley Griffin
beside koi splashing in bullrush pools
in a discrete outdoor room
in the foggy ephemeral sculpture garden of The National Gallery
we drank champagne
for the day, for all our yesterdays
and the gradual onset of tomorrow.

The sun beat down, I stretched toward it
As you two beneath an enormous green market umbrella
took refuge from the broad gravel avenues and grasses.

In the gallery I stood transfixed
before a vast brooding Kiefer landscape
Germany before, during, after
the war, the rain, the twilight
of the west

while you impish in a newfound
motorized chair came tooting by.

XI. Last Snapshot

In the photographs you gaze at the camera,
one hand on your new straw hat
the other firmly on your handlebars.

The sun blinks, the shutter clicks
The moment captured.
>   A rock garden with water
>   Masses of yellow potentilla
>   Clouds of pale purple ground phlox
>   Orange and coral bougainvillea stretching
like lichee nut branches across the frame.

If I could capture forever that moment
You almost in motion
     leading us on
If I could stay the shutter's click
     hold the sun, still the axis
what better time than now
when your blithe spirit calls,
Come on, let's go.

II

Divagations on Snow/Fall

The Mouse in the Cinderella Pageant

For Marty Gervais

It began with the road apples
it was a country town
and the milkwagons came down from Silverwoods Dairy
at the top of Canterbury street
and there were horses snorting in the cold air
and exhalations
and urictations
and the stirrups of the wagons were strapped on like shin guards
with leather traces
and pads, and blinds on their eyes.

The milk would be frozen and the cream top bulging out
from under the cardboard sealer
in the glass bottles at the back door

and the boys would go out
with their sticks and their brooms
and whackwhacka whack
and the banks of snow were tall
and fresh
and we shivered
our lips blue

but it was good for us we knew
the fresh air
the bright cheeks
and the ice-cold milk waiting
just inside the outside kitchen door.

There is something about the arena
at the back of the firehall
it's cold there too
and the boys are strapping on their pads
and putting on their helmets
and everyone wishes for a dime

for the hot chocolate made with water
and the little girls shiver in their wood-plank dressing room
while the boys go out and switch about, cutting up the ice
with their broad blades, and the parents sit up on the bleachers
drinking the chocolate water
rooting for their boys, who swish by in helmets and sweaters,
banging their pucks against the boards
slap into the net, against the goal posts
against the huge gloves
and caged eyes of the goal

and then the moment of enchantment
when the ice is cleared
and a waltz of some kind rattles over the tinny speakers,
and a stream of little girls emerges from their chilly lean-to
little limbs shake in the fawn tights, forming a line
and they begin to follow the lead girl,
who is more golden than the others
around and around the ice, cut up by the boys
trained on road apples, on canter buns,
the girls skate back wards and for wards
their little pony tails dance,
bangs bow, pirouette, twist, fall, and it's up again

the first magic of being other,
the short skirt in tartan   cut in a complete circle
the little jacket, the gangly fawn limbs
the flip of bangs, and toss of tail.

I'm there too, of course, one of the mice in the Cinderella pageant
the cold war has begun, the boys are eager to take the puck
all the way from southern Ontario to Korea.
It's not our war but we wish it were, think it is,
and we all shiver and make lists:
Mirror, mirror, on the wall,
Who's the fairest of them all ?

There are no parents watching the mice
in their little silver blades
it's gender territory and mice are
only brooches on the pads of guys in Charles Atlas costumes
and none of my brothers is out on the ice— no way
in a sensitive family
boys play music, and write
and fight their way outside of road apple territory.

After the rehearsals for pageants and hockey
there was always Lamont's bakery,
and the snow, the snow   by the side of the road,
by the side of Main Street
the snow on the way to the baker, to Lamont's bakery
and the snow in the alley with the horses at Dawes Bakery
where faun-haunched Peter Dawes, the town idiot,
locked the little girl in the stable
fondling road apples on his mind
after the games of road apples
after the chocolate water

the mouse in fawn tights
crosses her legs and lines up
and the donuts there so big
and the road so long and the snow at the sides
so high, and no other day was quite like that day,
or so the poet said, or so the poets say

a moment for a deal, a little coin exchange
the donuts were so big, the snow was so high
the sugar was so sweet
the buns so hot
and outside the door the steady stream of pee
while the boys trooped by
road apples on their minds.

And only a moment until
Bill and I, in his old red MG TD,
unlike any other car on the road apple road,
were bouncing its wooden frame down those country lanes
in road apple land off the skyscrapers of snow.

You think this is where it all ends
the country mouse
in her fawn tights,
her sensitive brothers, like cruel stepsisters,
but that isn' t the way it went at all.

Only Daughters

That last weekend I saw my mother
we went to the small market—
down near Beaver Lumber
where the public frozen food lockers used to be
high up in the sawmill warehouse—
and ate fat homecut french fries.

We didn't speak of our three month separation
though that had been our plan
nor of her illness, though she said
she was prepared,
we just hung out, me chauffering, suppered together,
lunched the next day

and then I went away.
My dog was with me, as usual,
and she's a bad dog, very charming,
always an unspoken friction
between me and my mother, whom
dogs adored, like loads of others,

but getting old meant she had begun
to shut down the portals for animals
and small children, and mess, and change,
and maybe her only daughter, but
we'd managed one last weekend
to lift the shades

chatted about this and that
my brother Robin's girlfriend,
who knew immediately how to load the new dishwasher
or my friend Jaquie's daughter who brought her tulips
or her neighbours who always called, so kind,
and my brother Steven's regular Sunday evening

telephone call, and the ticket she sent him annually

so he could fly two hours from Halifax, once a year,
no problem. I got into my old black Honda,
which had failed in the night from the cold,
and backed out of her garage. She was standing by the door.
The wind whistled, the walk slippery with ice. It was Sunday,

some of her neighbours were still at church.
I headed to the highway, back to my row house, my books
and my own garden still buried beneath the snow.

Cherries in Snow

The Man in *The New Yorker* ad
shows cherries in the snow

seated on a folding wooden chair
scarf tied in a knot at his neck;

he holds a single cherry by the stem
in the fingerless glove of his left hand

and in his right a simple wooden bowl
brimming with fruit.

He leans back on the chair
boots barely laced, legs splayed—

a good cap on his head.
He is looking out at us.

Contented, conspiratorial smile
under dark beetling brows.

A friendly face, intelligent
shrewd but not unwelcoming.

The snow is white, a few trees
visible in misty distance near horizon.

An admirable open tweed top-
coat, ditto knitted sweater.

He is wedged right at the front of the magazine
just after a photograph of Ralph Lauren
advertising his own American- Made In England
Purple Label Collection.

Cherry-man has slipped in to *The New Yorker*
just before the Table of Contents

which this month, September,
and not winter as in his photograph,

features men in blue and asks
Are we too hard on cops?

Should we take the kids out of the jails?
What really killed Princess Di ?

Is the new Getty Art Centre too good for Los Angeles?
Can technology set Tibet free ?

And so, with a kind of crazy piety he holds his piece
leans back

offers us cherries in winter
peaches in spring.

It's not about weather,
it's packaging.

And for that he'll answer to the world.
                            You bet.

Alexandra Park

I met a man with a bag of walnuts, a big bag,
the other day, the day before All Hallow's Eve
as I was walking my dog, in Alexandra Park.

He told me a story you won't believe. Well, maybe you might,
a story about squirrels, the squirrels in Alexandra Park
and other squirrels too. It goes something like this—
just a minute, I better set the scene,
It's autumn, fall, and the leaves have come a' tumblin' down
The park is loaded with leaves and squirrels:
they're mainly black against the yellow of the leaves
No red leaves here, sugar contents kinda low in a park
where the homeless hang out. Or is it ?
I'll get back to that.

Anyway, I enter the Park from the north—
on this particular day, west of the Tennis Court
on a diagonal down toward the subsidized housing development.
Lucy, the dog, made a big arc, stretching south and east of me.
Black squirrels streaking to tree-trunks
as white dog comes streaking through.
There are a lot of tree-trunks in Alexandra Park,
I ought to know,
I've been counting those trunks for eight years.

Some have got big holes in them, some are rotten,
and a few have disappeared.
And there are a lot of kinds of tree-trunks in Alexandra Park:
Poplars and catalpas, Manitoba maples and silver birches
Norway maples and elms, silver maples and oaks
and ashes and lindens, and chestnuts,
crabapples and honey locusts
a regular arboretum, just like the Park.

So I cut a diagonal into the Park

and stop on the edge of the baseball diamond
right near the empty wading pool and the waterfountain.
I began to halloo for the dog way over there on the volley-ball-Tai Chi court
and she came running by heading toward the paved arbor —
the walk which lines the east side of the outdoor swimming pool,
and the east side of the Park.
I was standing close to the empty wading pool as she ran by
and I looked over the park
and everywhere I looked were black dots—
moving dots, some running, some seated upright chattering,
all displayed on this enormous carpet
of soft luminous yellow pads.

A man in his late middle years—a sandy man
with a few sparse beige hairs on his head,
some, a few, beige teeth, beige skin
a sandy cardigan buttoned over a beige shirt
light brown trousers, brown shoes—
couldn't see his socks—
was standing holding a big beige paper bag,
and slowly picking out of it, one by one,
a big beige nut—a walnut
and tossing them—one by one
at the squirrels
in the sandbox, on the swings, on the see-saw
in the empty wading pool.

There sure are a lot of squirrels, I said
Wow, here she comes,
as Lucy, my dog, ran up.
This is her kind of day. I began to laugh
as she took off after another squirrel.
He looked alarmed.
His face wrinkled up a bit,
wrinkled that sandy smooth skin.
I hastened to reassure him—
She never catches them, though —
mind you she did once

Did she bite it?, he asked quickly
No—no—I said, She was surprised —
catching them's not the idea—
chasing them—it's a game.
She was astonished —and just let it go.
No, she's not a killer, he said, I can see that,
but some dogs are.
Well, the Park keepers told me
they wished the dogs would kill the squirrels.
They have no natural predators, and look,
every year, there are more of them.
That can't be true, he said, the squirrels control themselves—
some years there are lots, other years not,
they come and go, and each has a territory
you can see them —look—
chasing each other off their territories.

I looked a little sceptical and he began in earnest.
I feed them, and they know, and they leave their own territory to be fed
but they always go back to their place, their territory.
No—I can't believe the Park Attendant said that.
I report the killer-dogs, you see, I have to.
You know—and he paused —he looked a bit alarmed,
his forehead quite wrinkled—his eyes staring,
his right hand stilled, in the large bag of walnuts held on his left palm
What was I—I forget what I—I—oh, yes
You know nature has a way,
in the fall the sap goes down, down into the ground
and some of those trees have big holes in them,
not all—some, and those squirrels go into the holes—
there's two or three in a hole, and they curl up together in a ball
and they warm the tree up, when it's cold
So you see, nature has a way.

Bet she wouldn't like a walnut, he said.
Not unless you crack it open for her.
There, you see, those squirrels can crack them open.
I laughed and said, as I began to move off,
but she can eat a bone.

I thanked him for his story, told him I hoped
he had a good day, feeding the squirrels
and I began to walk over toward the pathway,
overhung with trees and bushes,
and paved with empty blue glass bottles of
Chinese Cooking Sauce from the People's Republic of China,
38% alcohol, a little salt and water, for only $1.15.

The dog had disappeared under a bush
although I could see her white coat
in among the dense foliage and branches
A man in a brown leather coat with a full black beard
and black dreadlocks, a man I see every day in the Park,
said hallo, asked me who I was calling on the empty pathway
Just my dog, I said, and called again.
And he said, I play music
I know, I said, I heard you yesterday
Was I good?
Yes—you were—there were a bunch of you
and one man was dancing and singing rap
and you, and a bunch of others, were beating on the bench
with drumsticks, and you were singing back-up, and you were beating,
and you were in the lead. You have a nice day, he said,
as the dog went up the path.

We veered left toward the corner of the indoor swimming pool
several of my neighbours were hanging about the orange steel double-fire-door
on the south wall of Scadding Court Community Centre
On the ground was a rice-cooker, several cases of coke
a couple of cartons of dim-sum buns, some bok-choi in plastic
and a lot of hidden goodies in stacks.
They were all old, rheumy-eyed and grey-haired,
all in slacks, all waiting
I said hello—they stared
as the dog and I walked up the path—past the jungle-jim,
the slides and ramps and picnic benches
to the Sanderson Branch of
The Toronto Public Library.

In Toronto With You

(After James Fenton, for Sam Solecki)

Don't talk to me of love, I've had a wombful
And I get wilful when I've gulped a glass or two.
I'm one of your love survivors
I'm imprisoned. I'm stranded
In Toronto with you.

Sure, I'm shocked at the ways I've been snorkeled
And astonished at the messes I've been through
I admit I'm permanently on the rebound
No matter where I'm bound
In Toronto with you.

Do you mind if I skip Niagara Falls and the McMichael
Give a pass to the Chinese lions at the ROM
Don't pat the pelvises on any stone camels
Say sod off to the sodding AGO
Spend all my time at home.

Let's stay as we are
By telephone
Sending messages to and fro
Unlearning who we were
Unlearning who you are
Learning who I am.

Don't talk to me of love. Let's talk Toronto
The territory that lies between our beds
There's a Vietnamese video arcade around my corner
And an old Jewish market up the road
Streetcars clang by Parliament buildings
And birds harikari on the Hydro's glass walls
That's Toronto, on line between our heads.

Don't talk to me of love. Let's talk Toronto

Toronto without anything from you
Toronto with your notes, your jokes, your promises
Toronto with...all of your affairs
Are you reading me? I hope so
I'm in Toronto with you.

Your Large Nose Etcetera

(After ee cummings)

My friend georgie didn't
want to poke her nose etcetera
in etcetera but during my recent
love affair could and what is more
did
tell me just what a
love af-
fair was

for
my brother sam thought
that all English men were
etcetera and made scores
etcetera and scores of etcetera
telephone calls not to mention
surprise visits invitations
since he knows
just what a love affair
my sister sue hoped that
i'd emerge
intact of course and
knew that i'd know
just what i'd been missing
mean

while I
was home alone
lying
in my bed etcetera
thinking of your eyes, crooked
teeth, smile
jokes, large
nose etcetera

and everybody knows
just what a big Nose
is good for.

III

Summer Altitude

The Massing of the Elk

1.

On the asphalt just beyond the path into the colony this morning, a large female elk. Arpeggios and scales float on the air between the music huts. A violin tunes itself. A soprano voice runs again and again aground on the same note. Bass piano chords respond higher and higher up into the treble. Dialogue becomes duet, becomes dissonance. Out of nowhere a cadenza appears. Deeper in the forest of scrub pine on the edge of the colony's pathway in the long soft bright green grass, peacefully chewing their cud, lie two chestnut elk, tails tipped with black. They rotate their soft periscope ears toward me, then, turning their long velvet brown necks, stare toward the path. For a moment my heart races, poised in the possibility of their standing, and then I move slowly on down the path through the dark density of the glade into the pool of noon light which encircles my star-shaped octagonal studio.

Toward evening, elk pods appeared everywhere in the colony. Yearlings and newborn cluster together tended by a single mother elk. In the darkest of glades not far from the colony bridge, several solo females meander at fodder, In the shelter of scrub, one chestnut beauty displays her soft beige rump, while lying on a bed of moss. I begin to creep through the underbrush, every exit blocked.

Toward dawn, thunder and lightning. At 5 a.m., I start to dress, eager to get to the studio to work. Then a sudden flash, and the power goes out. I stand in the darkness of my room in Lloyd Hall, looking out toward the mountains, wrapped in dense white fog, and down toward the asphalt agitated by the falling rain. In a few minutes, the power returns, lights all over the adjacent corridors visible through my window, and on the hillside. By 5:30 a.m., the woods are bright, and the ground shines with the freshness of morning and rain. A long single call from a blue jay pierces the solitude, a squirrel chatters in response, and I pick my way, down the path, to Studio 5.

2.

Crested Fawn

beyond my balcony
lying in a stand of pine,
dappled by late afternoon light
ears begin to twitch, large as her head
open up, move about
she attempts to rise
placement, arabesque
on spindly legs
sways a bit,
then up on all fours
ears continue to move,
scan the woods
a shift of weight,
attitude,
she crooks her rear right leg
balance off a moment
then, shakily, crooked leg
rises and moves
back to trumpet ear
white tail lifts like a flag
over soft white fuzzy rump
happily scratching
black velvet nose wrinkling
with pleasure.

3.

Two Jack Lake

High hot day
heat snakes up my filtrum
splits   nostrils
through sinuses, behind eyes
up into forehead and cortex
hot aromatic rush
of pine, spruce, juniper
and dry earth.

That other day
was wet and cool
The lake   green, emerald green
or even deep turquoise
It had been raining for a week.
The grasses grown up
lush, soft, green
covering the steep hill.

A mallard swoops low over the lake
wings in a haste of flapping,
doubles itself in water
rising to take the morning light.

4.

Notes on a Revelatory Experience which Transports

long phrase, brings a pause
through which elk rushes down incline
after newly-born babe
pursued
by a mummer's man
costumed with broom waving
bright yellow
plastic bag.

5.

Dancers in the Studio

Each body single, sculpted
as piano utters
melody, rhythm
body memory
imprinting,
tearing, welling
tears.

6.

Meridian
Sunday Sighting

Through the trees, scrubby pine
outside my window
on the ridge
a male baby deer, colour of fawn
fuzzy antlers like lichee nut branches,
or bittersweet,
grazing in the hill's fresh grass
delicacy of legs
dancers in studio
spires of grey trunks
grounded by bush
he leans his slender jaw down
black nose visible
above soft green fodder
at his rear, the white of fuzz
every muscle in that tiny frame
every bone visible clear
he turns and ripples
beneath delicate fluff
silly white tail   tipped in black
whisks
descends the rift
hightails it toward my studio window
light increases down
toward the noon meridian
Then he is gone
to another window
spindly legs, and soft prehensile ears
carrying him along the ridge
to another patch of fodder
another shaft of light.

7

The Massing of the Elk

Always a blur of soft brown
at the edge of my line of vision
only a moment ago an elk and her babe
on the far side of the road.

The squirrel on the balcony raises its tail
calls me to attention with its sustained chatter
each hair on a shivering alert.

It is scarcely two p.m.,
light has flooded my table
from the pyramid of sky—
a passing car blocks the view
as I think of Ariadne
and Theseus and the Minotaur
as I look for the mother elk
find her again, find her baby,
and you.

On the balcony an acrobatic squirrel
climbs up the wire balustrade
extends paws toward the mesh bag of bread
the bag begins to twist
the rear claws grip the wire
the front paws hold on, now, hold on,
as small jaws tear away
morsels of crust.

A short time before darkness
a visitor comes picking her way
out there, up the rift

She mounts the ridge,
small nose projected

through the verticals of trees —
lower branches, almost bare,
curl down.
Fastidiously, she rises
borne forward
on slender, tenuous limbs
framed by her mother,

and I sigh, for it is nearly eight p.m.
nearly time to shut down my computer
to pick my way carefully
out of the colony
toward the fourth floor lounge
I know they're headed in the wrong direction,
my direction, and that
if I leave my balcony
and my balcony glass doors
I'll meet them again
right at my front stoop.

So I wait a little longer
hoping to give us all
the grace of private passage
when up the rift comes
another and another and another
all legs and wobbling
battement, tendu, grand frappé
all forward movement
passing right and left
wake cut by prow
of plank-floored balcony.

So I save my document
eject my disk,
shut down my computer
and give myself over
to a contemplation of the view
out my screened front door.

I begin to count the mass in the forest
at the edge of my stoop
beyond the newly lit path.
First two adults, three babies;
then a third
and another young elk.
And I begin to worry for the unattended baby
In a moment it is over, united,
four mothers, four babies
a pride of elk.

I return to my studio,
gather my papers
worried now about biography
in the fourth floor lounge.
Better to think of these elegant creatures
gathered at dusk to lead me
Better to think of myself as a character
in a drama coordinated
by D.H. Lawrence
and these elk.

8.

Miracle of Morning

Two fawns
prance en pointe
perform a pas de deux
arabesque of white
suspended from black tip of tail
jet by my window
pirouette
tour en l'air.
They slide, one after another
up the rift, down the crease
toward the road,
pause among pines
ears like rudders   steering them up rise again
left of my deck:
no time for attitudes, it's all
legs up, batterie,
high step, pirouette
turns in the air.

With one grand leap the mother elk arrives
black legs sharp against soft green grass
stares at my window
as her rich brown calf comes bounding up—
it begins with the cabriole in the ravine
scissors of legs beating before rows of pine trunks
then a braiding, weaving, the entrechat,
as she rapidly mounts the rise
and lands with a fouetté, a grand whipping,
then tranquility
beneath soft belly   grace
butts for a nipple,
as two fawns abandon her
spotted rumps veer high toward highway,

tag-playing   all the way
Another brown calf appears in the forest
just as I search for a sign
type the word Forum, think assemblé,
look up from my computer
fecund female nose
pressed at port.

Today, it is summer in the mountains, and the elk and the deer
are nowhere to be seen. Out there, at Two-Jack Lake, I've passed
through a score of Dahl sheep, with thick curved horns,
still wearing part of their scruffy winter coats, looking a little unshaven.
I'm peering now through the forest of tall pine trunks beyond my balcony
hoping to catch sight of that flash of rich chestnut
that lets me know they're out there, waiting, watching.
It's the journey from Everlasting to Everlasting, from the Nay to the Yeah,
from the absolutely would not, to the might be, to the may be, to the could,
familiars leading beyond the labyrinth of memory
beyond the cortical forest

two mother elk at ground
one ear forward, one ear back
on either side of my prow.

IV

The Caverns of Ely

THE CAVERNS OF ELY

In 1942, a Treasure Trove of Roman silver was found on The Fens.
On the Great Dish, a sea-god with large staring eyes.
Four dolphins emerge from the wild locks of his hair.
The daughters of Nereus sing to the beasts of the sea.
Bacchus naked holds aloft a bunch of grapes.
Maenads, Satyrs and Pan whirl in a dance about them all.

1.

I will tell you a story of flatland,
never stable,
came from the sea first,
carcasses of sea creatures
corals, fossils, shells
stalk its soil.
    Men who dwell here
breathe air and water,
are amphibians,
half animal, half fish,
plough fields, drive lorries,
walk roads, pace hedgerows,
nestled beneath their trousers,
lie vast tails,
              and pulsing fins.
Softest tissues in bony-plated armour
gaps for mouths and eyes
and potent nether parts.

Surfaces twinkling like honey,
mermen of the Isle of Ely
bees buzz round their hives,
lush blackberries bend the boughs,
fields full of sweet sugar beets
and creamy-flowered potatoes.

Born from waterland,
these men hide their hearts,
honeycombed carapace cased
parts beckoning,
caveat emptor,
couple to perdition,
in stress secreting toxin,
the unique trunkfish.

Down, down, down, down,
See them as they rise
See the pearls in their eyes
Down, down, down, down,
See them   in the foam.

2.

High on the head where grows the branching apple
In a cavern pleasant, though involved in night,
Naiades delight, in bowls and urns
On which nymphs amazing webs display
And busy bees within secure
Honey delicious and nectar pure
Perpetual waters through the grotto glide
A lofty gate unfolds on either side
That to the north is pervious by mankind
The sacred south to immortals is consigned.

(Adapted from Porphyry, *Concerning The Cave of Nymphs*)

Whom would I tell whom the telling would not destroy?
    The heat in the blood that can not be cooled
caught unawares, surprised by love.
Is there, is there balm in the Gilead?
The one, the one beloved face
        borne by water
water always in your mind   unstoppable,

threatening the Great Ouse,
                   and its children,
       rising to flood the washes
whipped by winds ascending
breaking South   and Hillrow Fens
        washing over fields.
    Sometimes it is only a grey sea
swirling round Haddenham Hill.

Once in the umbilical cord of the Americas,
I met a trunkfish   lodged in a cove
He wooed me with tales of flatlands and horses
and led me to his garden grove.

        *   *   *

On the surface, it's just DNA combining
and recombining
         in finite fashion

         but enter and you
lose your bearings:
         what territory is here?
         where am I?
         what is that?

Another being's another
         planet, a jungle, a cave,
a sea grotto
of infinite extent,
     a quiet journey of the heart
pursued that we might love each other
and the world,
       better than we do.

Sirenia, ground zero, a manatee
hugs her pup, suckling
wreathed in sea-grass
doomed denizen, like

those others, hidden in caverns measureless,
crossopterygians, impossible name,
night-haunting creature
coelacanth, fringe-finned fish,
Latimeria Chalumnae, father/
mother, ready to walk,
but above or below, all doomed.

3.

Danger of language, echo of heartache
Whom might I tell whom the telling might not destroy?

Today, the first snow since you have gone
The garden vibrant with large, soft flakes
I sit at the window
                of the small guest room
looking out, looking at the flakes
Thinking of you.

*   *   *

It's nine o'clock in rainy England
Lonely, lonely, lonely forever
hard-hearted, heart-broken
                    kings of the sea.

Moonlight in Haddenham
one star alone alight
                above old grey steepleless church
all around lie fens,   fields
slope away into distant
                ship of the fens.
Wind blows, always.

Against the panorama of gold,
of grain, of green, of sugar beets

of red of lettuce,
against these are the horses.

The men have long gone to work,
The village stretches itself awake
tractors move along the road
a baby cries next door
like a ball bounced
                down steps.
        On Station Street, bunches
of yellow mums, pink carnations,
packets of tart, oval-shaped purple plums
appear on side tables
by High Street houses
        Rough signs beg passersby
for 50 pence   through letterboxes.

Summer of the great drought
on the fens is water, water everywhere.
        Wind rattles village gates
setting clicking stalks of grain
sound of Caribbean sea
or of gentlest Pacific latitudes,
                just at nightfall.

*   *   *

It's nine o'clock in rainy cold old England

Windmills dot gradually sloping bowl
beings at rest, forgotten
suddenly appear

to have always been there
in the realm of looming silence
of potential, of wind, of large wings,

rectangular, turning

awkward avatars, powerful of fen
land, waterland.

*   *   *

It's six o'clock in windswept England

Sweet spirit surrender to illusion
cheat expectation, sorrow of weariness,
on this enchanted ground
                a morning walk
no way too rough or steep
a velvet path scattered with rosebuds
fields bow to rim of horizon
blackberries and brambles bowl against old red brick walls
strengthened and refreshed
foreground
dense with petunias air their scent
pink bindweed nets the Gertrude Jekyll lavender
wind binds horses, churches,
tractors, windmills,
and beige claytile copping on the walls:
    Some had travelled like migratory birds,
others lived rooted to the earth like trees:
    Pensive Dido searching for the shade of forsaken Aeneas
waves her head and turns
toward the laughter of the setting sun.

*   *   *

Twilight at the gate on Bury Lane
the horse waits for me as light falls
sometimes it is alone
gentle at fodder in the parched field
three white socks stark against rich chocolate bronze.

One evening, he and I leaned against the gate
as light fell like coins tossed over shoulders
halfway across the field the dark one stood

nose to nose with a strawberry palomino mare
Moving toward us, sunset on their backs
already lord of the pasture at two,
part shire, part thoroughbred,
bronze Shylock nuzzles out five year old Crystal.

4.

Foliage and mood mark the seasons
temperature clarifies states:

> I'm shivering, it's winter
> I'm sweating, it's summer
> I'm ecstatic, it's spring
> I'm melancholy, it's fall.

*   *   *

It is fall
There is the drama of the skies, not forgettable.
Even now, evening, well past eight p.m., moving clouds
cross a vast darkening
                    grey and white and blue canvas
Narrow half-moon slit hangs in the immensity
                    of blue and white and grey
         at the top of the wooden gate
beneath clay and brick course.
    Against the rustle of leaves,
it is a sea I gaze upon.
I am the Hanged Woman. In bliss,
Hanging, horsed, I must be so.

Once a woman went so far she reached the place
where sky touches earth
bumping her head against sky,
she bent down and ate earth and tasted sea.

Down down, down down
See them as they rise

See the pearls in their eyes
Down down,
Down down,
See them down in the gloom
    Mermen of Ely's Isle.

        *   *   *

This high place is really an atoll garden
Lavender, its predominant moment
all shades, chakras, imagined
six-foot petunias, masses of violet-
           edged Pampas grass
Newton's prism fixed at its extremities
cast over the village's fuchsias, pinks
violets, indigo
        cut by yellow, orange and white.

        *   *   *

Sky turns an articulate grey
shaded, defined, moths start:
    Should I go out into the shadow;
dare I venture into the shadow of the night?

Is there anyone to whom I might speak
whom speaking would not destroy?

Beneath The Three Kings Public House
in Haddenham-on-the-Hill,
highest village in the fens,
lie Love and Innocence:
    Speechless Passion
by his bed kneels Faith
    He-warrior cradles spear,
                knife, shield boss,
iron buckle.

Vainly Faith attempts to woo him
to domesticity
flashing amber glass and silver beads,
soft her homespun tunic drapes
bright her bronze brooch glitters
fine her arched brows beckon
hands extending tweezers,
and bone
          spindle whorl
of spinning wheel.

5.

When she came upon the sea, she began to cal the gods and goddesses who
were obedient at her voyce. For incontinent came the daughters of Nereus,
singing with tunes melodiously: Portunus with his bristles and rough
beard, Salita with her bosome full of fish, Palemon the driver of the
Dolphine, three Trumpetters of Tryton, leaping hither and thither, and
blowing with heavenly noyse: such was the company which followed Venus
marching towards the ocean sea.

(From "The Marriage of Cupid and Psyches," *The Golden Asse of*
Apuleius)

This land is a seascape—
but I've told you that before—
the sea runs under the land
and in the ditches courses water
higher and higher in catch basins,
higher   than the land.
     There are fens here and bogs
          and the peat dries down
there is the Ouse, and the Greater Ouse,
the Cam and the Lark,
veins, twitching nerves
on the skin of landscape
to the north and the west, the canals of Wisbech,
to the north and the east, the cliffs and flats of Norfolk,

to the south and the east, the treasure of Mildenhall,
and north by north, The Wash.

People here speak differently than other places
shaded Roman imperators,
Gallic mercenaries, Greek rhetoricians
shadowed ancient Britons:
watery highways, land/language always moving.

Down down down down
See them as they rise
Beware the gems in their eyes
Down down down down
Foam-borne men   of Ely's Isle.

*   *   *

Once in the elbow of the Americas
I met a merman who led me to a grotto
                at the end of a spit
on the beach were the carcasses of his companions
killed in the great sea wars
starlet corals, tube corals
leaf corals and giant brain corals
staghorn corals, sea urchins
and enormous sea-potatoes.

Once they attached the head of a manatee
to the tail of a salmon
and called it a merman
Count Walkula, he height:
You can picture this, can't you ?
—but perhaps I've told you this already—
forgive me if I repeat myself,
it's hard to remember, it was, you see,
long ago when these wars began
           One must proceed slowly
always a fear of stuttering

existential mathematics lesson
degree of speed directly proportionate
to intensity of forgetting.

Beach of shells and corals
reef visible at the breakers not far offshore
masses of slender white herons fishing
scrub bushes, where no birds sing.
    Through the silence of the sandy path
ride a man and a woman
through the swish of bushes and depending branches
the path is dark with foliage
and silent
for a sudden moment light of floodlands
and fishing herons
                then thick scrub again
Sometimes the man leads,
and sometimes it is she
the sandy track narrows up an incline,
stopped by a barrier of bush
they are at the point:
beyond, in the sea, a fishing factoryboat
drift nets cast for miles
just before the gleaming reef.

Watch them and imagine
on the seashore, they might delay all day
and plan
how to love, and perchance then
sail away:
    she to the high Himalaya
he by the Maltese sea to complain
They could love light years until the drought
snuffed their fragile plan out.

Between her legs   the universe opens,
maenad with a tambourine,
nereids ride the waves, mounted on sea-beasts
Island of the Blessed
Journey of the Soul
Oceanus watches a longshore current
carrying her far beyond the jetty
    far away to the extreme
                        of light and sky and earth
stretched rip current rip
surge and surf.

Down down down down
See them as they rise
Beware the brightness of their eyes
Men of the sea, of Buckfast bees
Cold resistant, mite resistant
Abbots of surge and rip of tide.

6.

They told me if you found yourself at The Wash at dawn
and looked down, down in the deep clear water
you would see them, the tritons,
riding the magnificent dolphins
the nereids supple, each on her own manatee,
their steeds plunge with the waves
the tritons hold the reins, beards and forks aloft
the nereids sing as the sun begins to rise.

    Sometimes The Wash is dark with fluvial silts,
the courtship moves down
deep deep below the plunging waves
to sea caves and walls of coral
green moray eels lift their cocky chins
someone holds a delicate spidery shrimp
            in the palm of the hand
clouds of clownish wrasses,

fluttering of blue, banded yellow of   regal black angel fish,
schools of red-banded parrot fish,
and dusky damsels,
rainbows, stripes, bands, honeycombs, spots and scrawls
        hints of yellow and aquamarine, and inky black
coloured transparencies softer than
                the stained glass of Ely Cathedral.
A porcupine fish enlarges herself in alarm
tiny fins beating in terror, eyes widened
A zebra eel slinks by   slips into small hole.
Lobster tentacles test the currents from shelter
A great grey   turtle rides the descending cold currrent
Tiny rib corals, deep purple, fluorescent pink
Soft coral puddles mimic pastures above.

If you pass this way, look but do not touch.
Underneath the peat, in the rows and ditches,
marshy Witham valley, Car Dyke, Reach Lode,
lurk kindred of the mermen of Ely:
        spotted scorpion fish, red fire sponges
        glass armoured bristle worms,
long-barbed spined sea urchins,
men of war, moon jellyfish, electric rays.

                    *   *   *

Down down down down
A parley I do crave
Gentle love, 'tis long since
        methinks these wars begun
A truce I beg, and free conditions
  I do offer thee, since
vanquishing me,
        victory is mine own.

Triage, triage
I cannot put her whiteness from my mind
her hands scrabbling for the green grapes

her eyes rolling back in her head, or random moving
across the surface of her powdery moon face.

Smile creeps from mouth, moves over cheeks,
face turns up, head turns over
to meet the visitors that it greets,
to deny that you are there,
                    and I beside you:

Triage, triage, it's 3 o' clock in sunny Canada
in humid Toronto, poised on its own
vast inland   fresh water sea.

Stay, stay, stay, stay,
 arrest it in its rising.
Tide surging, current-carrying
        Faraday cage.
    A man's claws emerge,
clutch live lines, complete
circuit, hot wired,
a webbed, spider-
        man, rising, body electric
up, up the body electric into circle magnetic,
field draws him up, up in the wire cage
Omphalos, the navel of this, of other,
a baited web, exquisite array
        his giant metal claws
move out, out from my mind
toward live lines,
grid electric, holds landscape,
        holds world,
isolate
            forever:
man in the Faraday cage.

His movements are graceful
The girls he does please
And my love he has stolen away.

There'll be no eel pie at Christmas, this year.

7.

Today, my sweet fish, I am ill.
I beg you, pack me off on a packet to Bombay
or mount me
                  on Shylock, lead forth with Crystal
let us rush through fields of Solomon's Seal
calling me Sheba,
                  erase my keen
Mayday, mayday, mayday.

If a man lived all day on iguana soup,
his brawn would match his brain:
an iguana's two penises
converse with a human's two brains
the stomach's enteric nervous system shelters
one-hundred million more neurons than the spinal cord:
the brain in the head, the brain in the gut
in constant comment.

*   *   *

It is a sentimental journey that we make
to the land where Holstein-Friesens
      joust with windmills
having been in love almost all my life
may I go on so 'til I die
for mean actions are surely the intervals
between one passion and another,
the interregnum where heart is locked up,
until rekindled,
            farewell generosity and goodwill.
      I would do anything for or with anyone
if it not be a sin
to divide is to lessen

to expose is to risk
to risk is to lose
love is nothing without sentiment
sentiment is always less than love
immerse it into the very ocean and it will stand
ocean fills mind with grand ideas

but you are too far inland from The Wash
and the fens are drained.
    To the great deep, a pail of water is a paltry thing
but that pail might be in the very next room
from the heart the blood depends to the wrist
lay but your two fore-fingers
lack-a- day-sical
on the artery to take the critical ebb and flow:
Are there not worse occupations than feeling a man's pulse?

And the winds from their eyes
Blow black windmills on the hills
And the waters rise
And the warriors surge
    in the surf
Foaming on horseback
    at joust on the turf.

8.

Three toads splashing in Nick's garden in the rain.
It is dark; it is evening in Hadnam
There was a summer drought and now there is autumn
nights enlarge themselves as skies discharge
Summer had its joys
and winter we hope might delight
but now it is autumn in Haddenham- on- the- Hill.

Our hour of remembrance has drawn close:
I see you, hear you, feel you
whatever comes,

72

someone clears her throat
the bluebird on the board fence
the horse in the meadow just beyond the close:
sometimes the moon is not such a perfect circle.

Man and woman circle one another
her private parts counterfeit the sea
tumbling in a froth of bed linen

A tree good enough to rot under,
wild blackberries just across the road
from the garden of The Cherry Tree Public House

*   *   *

With cross and legends   and legions of mermen
came Ovin to Ely's Isle
managed the land for Etheldreda
built the first church on the hill in Haddenham
buried with cross on a path of pumpkins
where Linden End meets Aldreth Road
        at Stonecross Farm.

Down down down down
See them as they rise
Shield yourself, the glare in their eyes,
See them as they sport in the foam
Hear them as they wail and moan
        Mermen of Ely's Isle.

9.

The wind came up strong today, when you were absent—
I wanted to say away, but feared the closure of a rhyme—
I felt the sadness in the wind, so much sadness in the wind,
and thought of sending cards inscribed to all whom I love
"It is very windy here",
                    as I gathered the laundry from the line.

Season of mist and mellow fruitfulness
another poet's words
pumpkins depend, sorrows are at end
another game of cards.

Since there's no help, come, let us kiss and part.
Nay, I have done, you get no more of me,
And I am glad, yea glad with all my heart
That thus so cleanly I myself can free;
Shake hands forever, cancel all our vows,
And when we meet at any time again
Be it not seen in either of our brows
That we one jot of former love retain.
Now at last gasp of Love's latest breath,
When, his pulse failing, Passion speechless lies,
When Faith is kneeling by his bed of death
And Innocence is closing up his eyes,
      Now if thou would'st, when all have given him over,
      From death to life thou might'st him yet recover.

"Beware the pairs", you wrote
duplicitous,
          hidden in flowers,
and little did I know,
'twas yet another game of cards.

              *   *   *

Flowered cushions, sea anemones
dark centres, floating threads, veins
opening bidding entry
hiding the unseen
      Outside the window, figures move
there is a sound of roaring water
                storm-towered waves
          woman wakes from a drift
by fire   outside gale,
guttering of two last candles—

someone has been stealing greyhounds in all the surrounding villages
recent building's panes rattle
    Wind roars
         like a great beast at window
let me in, let me in,
sometimes it dies down
feels it is over, ferocity subsides
and then above tractors' whine
combustion, again.

        *   *   *

Today, I am ill
      little better than an old woman
or a Dreamer of Dreams in scripture language
on the beaches of Hunstanton and Cromer we run our races
one wheel in the sea, the other in the undulations
      of the sand
    on your departure my heart broke
out wth blood
      to stain my handkerchief
the Beach even as a mirror where we met
and where I shall meet you on your return
    Once in Belize, we were sailors
I lay on your limbs in the wind
sail flapped about, sun beat down on
January love.
    So much unfinished business.
The drama is ripe, the theatre decorated
all thickets and grottos retiring   solicit our pledge
Blue hole of Belize, a striped canvas lunch
shades the bar's Queen
      Victoria's deathly silence.

Never love inconveniently
beware moonshine and starlight
spite its fearless ferocity,

love demands never
disturb your community
switch the switch for Ipswich
prevent a hitch, which is the switch
which you desire which I must switch to
know which switch is which.

Out before seven a.m., deadheading daisies
          diving at dahlias
dreaming of, lingering in
the sea, lest human voices wake
and we drown:

Down down down down
See them as they rise
See the pearls in their eyes
See the spines 'neath the skin
Beware the body electric
          Mermen of Ely's Isle.

Truce, gentle love, a parley now I crave !
Methinks 'tis long since first these wars begun,
Nor thou, nor I, the better yet can have;
Bad is the match where neither party won.
I offer free conditions of fair peace:
My heart for hostage that it shall remain,
Discharge our forces, here let malice cease,
So for my pledge thou give me pledge again.
Or if no thing but death will serve thy turn,
Still thirsting for subversion of my state,
Do what thou canst —raze, masssacre, and burn;
Let the world see the utmost of thy hate.
   I send defiance, since, if overthrown,
    Thou vanquishing, the conquest is mine own.
        * *   *   **

Doorway to the deep
Maenad with her tambourine
Oceanus unveils the view

Faith keyless at Passion's door
and then no more
                    the two.

There'll be no eel pie at Christmas, this year.

V

Scottish Borderlands

Hawthornden Processional

For the horses out in the paddock
on the walk down Polton Lane hill

we were backdrop. It was nine p.m.,
still light, for this is a northern place,

as we formed a ragtag against the
spare sleek beauty of the chestnut

and her colt. The hills were terraced,
crosscut, grades of green

a slight ripple in the gilding
of the wheat at evening.

And we cut down the gorge
deep into the valley of Polton

past De Quincey's cottage
to the chasm below.

I'd been reading Pinsky on poetry
and Proust on Sodom and Gomorrah

and was grateful for the descent
to green, to flowers, to stillness

and the running of the cascades
and for the puff back up the steep road.

We imagined as we climbed
that we were proprietors of all the grand

houses on offer on the seductive
charming road, and that we would

remain forever in Scotland,
near the Castle, hatching our poems

and stories, in endless good fellowship
a gang of North Americans suspended

in dirigible laden with cakes and tea
and fresh salmon and new-dug potatoes,

floating down the front staircase
on a breeze perfumed with bog flowers,

bearded regal purple irises, the palest
lavender phlox and the sharp white and

gold of orange blossoms reflected forever
in the mirrored copper preserving kettle.

But the road back was different.
The little two ups and two downs

of the housing development had disappeared
and there were spires everywhere.

Lupins and foxgloves and delphiniums
stretched their purples and blues

and whites and pinks up toward the soft
puffy cumulus clouded sky, weedy loosestrife

pointing them on higher and higher.
On every hillock, in every crease

of the soft sloping edges of the bowls
toward Bonnyrigg were horses, gentle

at fodder. Fields of orangey-red poppies massed
and swayed, and the hedges were high with pink

and white bramble rose, delicate elder
flowers, umbrellas of Queen Anne's Lace.

The clouds of poppies moved gently
as the horses shook their manes,

and we scuttled back bound in scarves and
baseball caps and headbands and keefiyahs

down the yellow broom-flowered Castle drive
with its towering oaks and sycamores,

poplars, Scots pines, yews and ashes,
down our small portion of the valley

of the North Esk, stopping only as a sinewy fawn
crossed flanked by two white-tailed hares.

Summer Rain

I spent part of the summer solstice
looking out of a bus window

on the rainy roads of Edinburgh
and the surrounds

haunted by snatches of old poems,
thinking of you.

I left the castle right after breakfast.
The rain began, not a bunny to be seen

and the bus came quickly to the gates.
Behind, my companions were still at table

exercising our special North American levity,
exorcising the castle's discipline

exercising the castle's administrator
who felt he held the New World's chaos at bay;

So they said Magellan on the Straits of Darien
overwhelmed by bright plumed headdresses

and all the chattering coloured beings
of a green frontier

lush, breast of promise, but here
too the leaves are dense

a fox moves his muscled shoulders
in the glen below

rooks mass in black nests
high up in the sycamore trees

and the horse paddock, and the railway trail to Bonnyrigg
are alive with poppies.

There was nothing special in Edinburgh
about the longest day of the year.

It was Gay Pride Day and despite the rain
the streets were festive:

Penitential nuns marched with barechested men
claiming perpetual indulgence

The shops after bristled with excitement
and the sun came out briefly

just as the parade finished. From Lawnmarket
I headed down George the IVth bridge to Victoria

then along Bow to the junction
of Cowgate and the Grassmarket.

I was hungry, very hungry
I wanted to eat. I wanted to eat

you. There was no moment of that long day
when I felt truly alone.

The babies' plump luminous cheeks
in the Cranach paintings on panel, the happy parson

profiled skating across the blue icy Raeburn surface,
the tumultuous fall of Niagara of Frederic Church.

I will consign myself to this edgy
companionability

To this dangerous yearning
from which I turn

To the contemplation of your shadow
formed by light in all the photographs

I carry everywhere in my mind.

Hawthornden Fire

Watching I learned a lot
    about the nature of fire

Placed one log, then another in the grate
Tucked in twists of old poems, scraps of tissue
body exuvia transferred to cast a hex on the flames

But the wood from the valley was too wet
with North Esk water
with rising damp from the rhododendron glen

And as the logs and knots sizzled on the hearth
over the odour of firelighter, under the mantel
laden with fruit and tea and words

the caverns and the dungeon and the secret passages
of the castle rose up in the smoke and sputter
of my gradually dying flames. I threw on more oil

a Lover's Loop appeared, then Wallace's cave
its entrance framed by brilliant violet viper's buglos
The far bank of the Esk lit with frostings of Queen Anne's lace

and the gentle Castle Walk's return was garlanded
in pink and in white rhododendrons, and slips of veronica,
the horse paddock alive with grand black stallions and the ondulations

of red and orange field poppies massed
like fragile clouds beneath the black caw caw cawing
of the rooks in the towering pines.

The fire flared up, stretched out exuberant
died down, and glowed
one a metaphor for human desire
the other for human love.

Herm On Tour

Concerning light and air he made no errors
Captain Fowke of the Royal Engineers
for sunny days cast a creamy world,
an airiness caught by terrazzo and sky
To meet the deluge that world transformed
to taut transparency, colossal ribs
stretched against the elements:
To look up is to look down

into a sharp-boned glass boat
flat keel like an arrow.
To look up is to float on the frame
of an invisible umbrella.
Everything about the scene is transposed—
a symmetrical face first launched
on a dreamy Venetian canal, gilded Moorish
cast iron canopy columns, three towering

storeys to the clouds, medieval decorative
crosses, rosettes, and clerestory
the foundation stone laid by Prince Albert
his last public appearance—
everything transposed and decorously
somehow in place. What song sang the sirens
to draw me back past that Italian Renaissance facade
past forecourt cases of ossified

whale penises and Scottish contemporary
ceramics, through the great glass hall
up the caged and netted stairs
over shallow fish pools alert
with massive sunset Chinese koi
forced by depth to turn amphibian
their backs rising to air, flitting
or floating sideways, a Cubist moment—

up to Middle Eastern markets hung with
narrative, past corridors of cymba molluscs,
black abalone, green turban, soft-
bodied invertebrates sinuous
curving mantles to a grinning Flemish
bison in a stand of oaks, transfixed
by Venus at her toilet in wool and silk.
    On the shoulders of four wind gods rises
a cup braced by a back-curving herm

leaning saucily in leafy apron
over the bowl like Narcissus yearning
toward the beautiful boy who blew him kisses
from a purple iris-fringed ferny pool.
From cream Saint-Porchaire ground he reaches
from garish polychromed Palissy landscapes
of salamanders and serpents, cockles and mussels,
chunky lobsters and frogs frozen in clear tin glazes

a latecomer to Edinburgh
a long journey from the Gothic
crenellations of Walpole's Strawberry Hill
its objects of virtu, its mushroom and
cream library, and endless basins
of stomachachey fresh strawberries and cream.
    The herm is ebullient as he steers his boat
to plant a kiss on his own figurehead

his deep golden curly hair wreathed in
triumphal glistening gold braid.
Four bald men with cuphandle ears
strain at the pitcher's belly
mouths open for a high C, or the wind,
a gilded Greek key frieze like an endless
summer wave holding them firmly
in their stocks.

Other herms appear, a duet of lions
harmonize on the E, a trio of
kings sing a D about the base,
a song of moulds, appliqué
punch, strap, and stamp
of rust lozenges, flowers and
leaves, gilded quatrefoils and
purple calligraphic arabesques,

Oriental tracery of green and blue on cream
suspended on the negative of bulge
transparencies released from earth,
design shaping bowl and not
contrariwise, as puffs of elder flowers
launch their leaves, or the cadmium
yellow broom its verdant bush.
    The herm navigates his shell

out, out of the case, out of the museum,
out of the town, past Arthur's Seat, south
to Rosslyn Glen, buoyed on the burbling North Esk,
banks open around the blue lips of his craft,
parting like the walls of the Great Hall
itself, his spirit's barque driven
far from shore. White puffs of
cumulus cloud sail against the blue-milky

disk of the sun, umber water purls over
ochre rock and fallen trees, pea-green ferns
reach tall against fuchsia of wild foxglove
and cobalt blue lupin, and pointed forest-green laurel
the light is strong, the sun hot
the Esk flows noisy beneath the cacophony
of birds and the distant cawcawcawcaw
of the crows.

Queen Anne's lace like giant white parsley
rises five foot in the air

like the creamy earth of Saint-Porchaire
stocks thick like rhubarb
softest melted streaky greens and cinnabar
sharp-edged papyrus grasses
and the leaves of day-lilies bent in arabesque
and on the far shore, no further

than the far walls of the Great Hall
are rosettes of white, a slope of ram's heads
at the base like miniature corbels
buttercups and white daisies and purple
clover flowers in the grass, alpine
strawberries from tiny plants depend
near the portals, as the tangled garden
of the glen, its pale frosted leafy curving canopy

its purling cinnamon waters, its clear brooks
tumbling over pathways, its brown trout
leaping round the vessel,
while the herm blowing kisses and smiling
rigs his sails, calls his crew
and to triumphal chorus
embarks to steer his ewer along Cowgate,
up to Chambers, home again.

To My Soul's Desire

In the tapestries the lady consorts with her lover,
the white unicorn in a ground of rich rose and blue.

I have been thinking constantly
of my journey to meet you.

First the white unicorn rests its hooves in her lap
while regarding its own face in a mirror.

Their companion, a lion, holds a banner
of three crescent moons.

I will go to Waterloo Station and get aboard a train
and go under the channel which separates me from you.

In the second, with her love on the left, and her strength on the right,
the lady plays a portable organ,

her heart a loudbeating, as her maidservant pumps a bellows.
I can not tell you how confused I am,

but I send you my love
as I contemplate your picture.

The lady reaches toward a lacquered box of sweetmeats
which melt in her mouth.

Her love reaches toward a tray of Turkish delight.
The lion embraces them with kisses.

I will pass under the water and arrive in Lille before noon.
You will come by land.

The lady makes a garland of flowers for her love's crown,
placing a kiss in each pink multifoliate bloom

of the soft sweet carnations.
I must come to you as we planned

though my impulse is to throw away my ticket
and to flee.

The lady lets her hands fall down
the sides of her lover's head.

She touches the delicate bones,
explores the sweet orifices

of the head,
then grasps the unicorn's horn.

All winter during my long illness,
I wrestled with our dark night of the soul,

until I purchased my passage.
Under the striped canopy, overlaid with a starry night sky,

the lady at last reaches her soul's desire,
the jewel of the soft pink velvet folded casket.